jonty lees

lodger

Introduction / Martin Clark, Artistic Director / Mark Osterfield, Executive Director

Jonty Lees is the fifth artist in the Tate St Ives Residency Programme to occupy Number 5 of the historic Porthmeor Studios. Lees works in video, sculpture and installation, but the stuff of his practice, his medium, is the world around him – the objects, images, memories and dreams that saturate our daily lives. For many artists the studio is a place set apart, a refuge from the clamour of the everyday. For Lees this very special studio – previously occupied by those giants of British Modernism, Ben Nicholson and Patrick Heron – came to exert an unusually direct, and perhaps unexpected, influence on his work.

Lees' approach to the blankness and silence of the studio was to reclaim the space as a part of the world. He rode his bike around in it; he dragged the outside in, filling it with stuff, dumping piles of leaves all over the floor before creating his own brisk, autumn breeze with a piece of 8 x 4' plywood; he kept himself amused in there with all manner of inventive distractions, diversions and play. On each of our visits to the space, often only days apart, it would always look entirely different: sometimes full of clutter, sometimes almost empty – new ideas and half-formed works would appear and disappear over a matter of hours, unable to keep up with the furious pace of his imagination.

It is from just this impatient state of distraction and play that Lees' works emerge. He has an incredible sensitivity to objects and materials, to their cultural, social and aesthetic histories. Whilst many of his works posses a disarming immediacy, there is a slowness, a willingness to pause, to linger

You and me (We'll always have Norwich) 2007 /
Bicycle inner tubes and puncture repair patches / Dimensions variable

over the apparently banal little miracles of the everyday: light on glass, the wind against skin, the beauty of a BMX or a French baguette.

But the affable nonchalance of many of his works belies a more insidious and irresistible engagement – snaring the viewer with their easy charm and catching them off guard. Amongst the quiet familiarity there lies a surrealist's penchant for the dream-like disjuncture of objects and images, of memories and fragments – an attraction to the unsettling and the absurd. Sigmund Freud knew that the uncanny was firmly rooted in the everyday, his term *Unheimlich* literally

Sunny Day 2007 / Video / Duration 00:28:00

translates as 'unhomely'. Lees understands this too. But his is not a clichéd nineteenth century pastiche, it is thoroughly contemporary (and therefore much more disturbing), located in objects that are almost invisible in their ubiquity.

For Lees the work is often just a way of elevating these everyday objects and emotions to a kind of perfect visibility, a way of recreating a moment, a memory or a feeling, refigured through the proximity and materiality of the *thing*. One thinks of Martin Creed's *Work No. 232* 'The Whole World + The Work = The Whole World'. Sometimes, in order to make something new, we need only give ourselves the time and the space to see what is already there.

We are enormously grateful to Michael Archer for his insightful and pitch-perfect essay in which he extrapolates on some of Lees' illustrious antecedents when it comes to 'mucking about in the studio', doing something when there's nothing to do, and always taking the long way round.

We would also like to thank Sara Hughes, Curator at Tate St Ives, for all her work and support on both the Residency Programme and the exhibition, as well as Matthew McDonald, Dave Davies and Simon Pollard for their considerable technical assistance and expertise.

This residency has been made possible with the support and dedication of the following organisations and individuals: Arts Council England, South West, and in particular Mariam Sharp; Tate St Ives Members, Tate Members; The Borlase Smart, John Wells Trust and University College, Falmouth. In addition we would like to thank the selection panel comprising: artist Ged Quinn; Susan May, White Cube; Ann Gallagher, Head of British Art, Tate; Virginia Button, curator and writer, and Susan Daniel McElroy, who as former Director conceived the programme in 2003.

Above all, our thanks must go to Jonty Lees for his extraordinary enthusiasm, commitment and exuberance in both art and life, and for his beautiful exhibition.

Tour de Studio 2007 / Video / Duration 02:45:02

page 9–11 **Untitled** 2007 / Video / Duration 03:18:15

You know, for kids! 2007 / Toy propeller, gaffer tape / 10 cm diameter

Energy Transfer / Michael Archer

At the beginning of *Civilisation and its Discontents* published in 1930, Sigmund Freud describes something like an archaeology of the mind. Imagine Rome, he says, a place where over the centuries buildings have been erected and destroyed only for others to rise and take their place. The mind is something like that. Things – ideas – are erected or constructed there, only for them to be superseded by the traces of further thoughts and experiences. The difference, Freud suggests, is that whereas in real life Rome there is an inevitable loss of coherence so that one has to reconstruct the past from fragments, in the mind nothing gets lost. All we need to do is to find the right way to recover or uncover it. This occurs to me as I sit on the knackered, collapsed sofa in Jonty Lees' studio. It's the same studio that has been used in the past by the artists Ben Nicholson and Patrick Heron, and it's the same sofa that those two must also have sat and relaxed on. It now looks like something that has been rescued from the skip more than once. It's appallingly uncomfortable. Maybe it didn't used to be.

The silly idea – which you want to resist, but which has its charm – is that simply by being in the studio one gains access to a history of art. Lees knows this is not true, but plays up to the conceit anyway in *Tour de Studio* 2007. When Nicholson and Heron were there they made paintings. The space was manifestly a place of manufacture, of hand-production. Canvases got stretched, boards got prepared, they were painted and were then shipped out to be shown elsewhere in galleries. But there is another aspect of art's history in which the studio itself and the activities that go on within it have become the focus of attention. One thinks of William Wegman in the early 1970s playing around with the then newly-available technology of the video camera. He wasn't using it to make epic cinema, just to film himself passing the time – twiddling his thumbs, perhaps, or doing crude party tricks with his stomach, or messing around with his two Weimaraners, Fay Wray and Man Ray. There's the series of photographs taken by Jan Dibbets showing the shadows shifting in an otherwise empty room as the sun travels across the sky outside. 'Look,' he seems to be saying, 'here's the evidence that I've spent all day in my studio. That level of dedication must count for something.' Then there's Bruce Nauman, filming himself, say, walking in an exaggerated manner round the perimeter of a square marked out on the studio floor; or walking round the same square playing a single note on the violin; or photographing a paint-spill on the floor, because if a studio is where art is made, then maybe everything that happens there, including the accidents, can be seen as art.

Half a century before Wegman, Dibbets, Nauman, and others there was, of course, Marcel Duchamp's first readymade. His 1913 work *Bicycle Wheel*, sits at the heart of this enquiry into the place of the studio in contemporary art practice. Full of contradictions, it first appears as a more-or-less straightforward sculpture on a plinth. And yet. The plinth is a stool, designed to be sat on when you want to remain comfortably in one place. But you can't sit on it because the bicycle – designed to be sat on when you want to move comfortably from one place to another – has been turned upside down and plonked on top. It stays still and it moves. For Duchamp the wheel's movement provided a gentle visual distraction while one was in the studio. In doing so, however, it posed the question as to whether distraction should now be understood as the behavioural mode essential not just to the studio, but to art and the world more generally. Rather than finding oneself occasionally distracted from the main task at hand, was it not now the case that one always functioned in a distracted state? Analysing the implications of the new importance of *Zerstreuung* (distraction) was the cultural philosopher Walter Benjamin's aim in his famous

1936 essay, *The Work of Art in the Age of its Technical Reproducibility*. He begins section 13 of the essay with this observation:

'It is inherent in the technology of film, as of sports, that everyone who witnesses these performances does so as a quasi-expert. Anyone who has listened to a group of newspaper boys leaning on their bicycles and discussing the outcome of a bicycle race will have an inkling of this'.

Tour de Studio, the humorous film of Lees cycling round this not overly-large St Ives studio where he has been working, draws all of this history into its orbit. In spite of this, it is implacably a work of the present. We can't ignore the fact that a decision to get on a bicycle nowadays speaks less to a Tebbit-like[1] search for employment in the late-industrial landscapes of Britain, than to an environmental concern that stretches well beyond these shores. The issue as to how far art can either engage with or contribute to this reality is signalled as one requiring serious thought.

There are two other bicycle-related works in a similar vein. In the first, *You Know, For Kids!* 2007 a small propeller fastened to a bike's handlebars becomes both a source of visual pleasure and a potential energy source. No bigger than those hand-held, battery-operated fans that never cool you down on a warm day, the propeller spins whenever the bike is ridden. It thus provides gentle visual incident in the periphery of the rider's vision while also acting as a micro-generator. Use and beauty at one and the same time. And that's before we've started to think about *le dopage*. The second, *You and me (We'll always have Norwich)* 2007 is an arrangement of two interlinked bicycle-tyre inner tubes hung on the studio wall as two overlapping circles. It's a small puzzle. To separate them seems such a simple task, yet it really can't be done without cutting and rejoining one of the tubes. The visual conundrum is akin to finding a pair of trainers tied together by their laces

1 As Employment Secretary in Thatcher's government, Norman Tebbit became associated with the slogan 'Get On Yer Bike' in reference to encouraging job seekers in the early 1980s to go out and find work.

and slung over a telegraph wire. Or coming upon a bicycle tyre around the base of a street lamp. How do such things get there? Was it effortless, or did someone spend hours throwing the things up until they got lucky? German artist Andreas Slominski, once celebrated the bizarre and excessive joy felt at such encounters by arranging for a gang of workmen to hoist a lamppost out of the ground. He then placed a tyre on the ground round the hole before having the post re-inserted. 'Why be simple if you can make it complicated?', he says.

This notion of distraction figures again in the kaleidoscope Lees has fastened to the bonnet of his car, *Teleidoscope* 2007. Not content with seeing the landscape as it scrolls across the car's windscreen, he has devised a means of making the view more varied and exciting. By allowing the driver to look through an arrangement of mirrors, the scene becomes fragmented and divertingly patterned. It might make concentrating on oncoming traffic a tad more difficult, but it will certainly deliver an exciting ride. In spite of appearances, though, the impulse is not to engage in extreme sports. It is to reckon with the extraordinary disjunctions that become evident when one examines the world from different viewpoints. It's always easy to slip up when we are looking at things. We can misinterpret, and we have to be constantly on the look-out to avoid mistakes. Father Ted knew this, which is why he was so careful to explain to Dougal the difference between things that are small and near, and those that are big and far away[2]. Paul Cézanne knew it as well, as he wrestled to integrate subtly distinct perspectives into a coherent spatial representation on the flat surface of his canvases. Lees' lenticular postcard *Casio* 2007 teases us into reckoning with this, too. Depending on how you angle it you will see either a watch or a blinding flash of light reflected off its glass. It's a version of the kind of thing that happens all

2 Parodies of Irish priesthood from Channel 4's 1990s cult TV show, *Father Ted*.

the time, and which, when it occurs, one often turns into a child's game. But to perform it for the purposes of making the card, Lees has had to take the watch off and sit at a table in order to hold it at the precisely correct angles for the necessary photographs to be taken. Once again an occurrence that is usually deemed worthy of nothing more than an amused and slightly dismissive nod of acknowledgement gets mixed up with craft, application, effort, and perseverance.

Why be simple if you can make it complicated? There's a length of rope lying on the floor stretching away from the sofa across the studio. Lees picks up the end nearest to him and waggles it up and down, setting up a wave that travels with ever-decreasing amplitude down to the other end. He suggests that this seems to have something to do with memory. Perhaps you could set up a machine to do the waggling and then everyone would be able to see it without him having to be there all the time to keep waving his arm. That might sound like a cop-out, but of course it would take a lot of time and resources and experimentation to make sure that the appropriate set-up can be achieved. Such a simple outcome would not happen without this considerable effort. Lees' work abounds with instances of this kind of confluence between economy and profligacy. He is captivated by the poet Edith Sitwell's remark that her family used the private term, 'through leaves', when referring to any effortless engagement with the opulent materiality of the world. A pile of leaves presents visual bulk, but parts before our stride without offering the least resistance. Similarly, it will scatter in the breeze made by a passing car. A heavy, lined curtain can glide easily along a smooth track, and so on. Importantly, the bulk of the leaves does not diminish, the weight of the cloth is not magically lessened. In each instance it is not that the resistances of the world are removed – as if one could deny gravity, for example – but that, rather, these resistances are seen to work against each other in a mutually supportive, almost symbiotic manner, and that in doing so one is given space to appreciate and enjoy the outcome. The pleasure to be derived from such encounters is, I think, closely related to Duchamp's idea of the *infrathin*. The *infrathin* is a space or a quality of the world whose existence we can intuit, but to which it is difficult to gain anything other than imaginative access. The examples Duchamp gives are the space between one side of a sheet of paper and the other, the 'taste' of smoke as it touches the mouth, or the slight rubbing between trouser legs as one walks. What we are talking about is nothing less than art. It is a response to the world that goes beyond mere instrumentality.

Part of what characterises this response is an understanding that the process is one of reciprocity. One is not imposing an attitude upon things seen so much as meeting them half way. At the same time as you turn your attention to them, they can be seen travelling in the opposite direction back towards you. Nothing is passive in this energised relationship, which Lees has literalised in his photographs of objects standing to attention when someone enters the room, *We salute you!* 2007. When unobserved, we must suppose, these sausages, baguettes, brackets and other assorted items hang limply on the wall. But as soon as the door opens they rise up to greet the newcomer. In his choice of phallic objects Lees is surely making a tongue-in-cheek reference to artists Peter Fischli and David Weiss's sausage photographs, and in his jerry-rigged system of strings and pulleys to the studio experiments seen in their film *Der Lauf der Dinge (The Way Things Go)* 1987. Once again, therefore, the question is raised in these images of just what it means to spend time in the studio. Their inescapable eroticism insists that the perverse behaviour which leads the artist to shut him – or herself away in order to pursue a half-idea until it either resolves into something substantial or falls apart altogether is fuelled, ultimately, by the desire to reconnect purposefully with what's outside the studio door. Lees' work shows that one powerful way to unearth the potential for thoughtful engagement between people – and between people and things – is to raise 'mucking about in the studio' to an art form.

We salute you! 2007 / Assorted objects, fishing wire, hooks / Dimensions variable

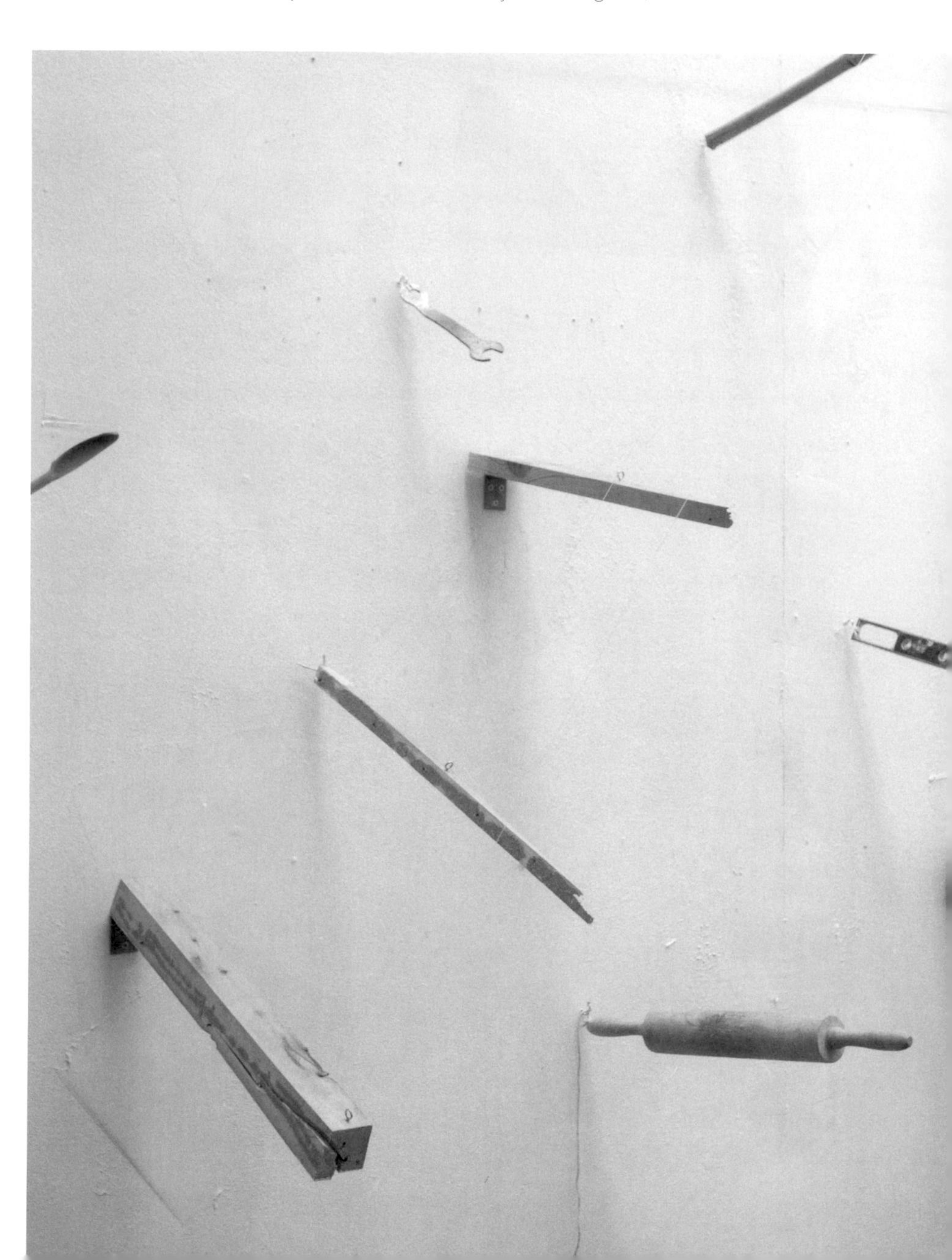

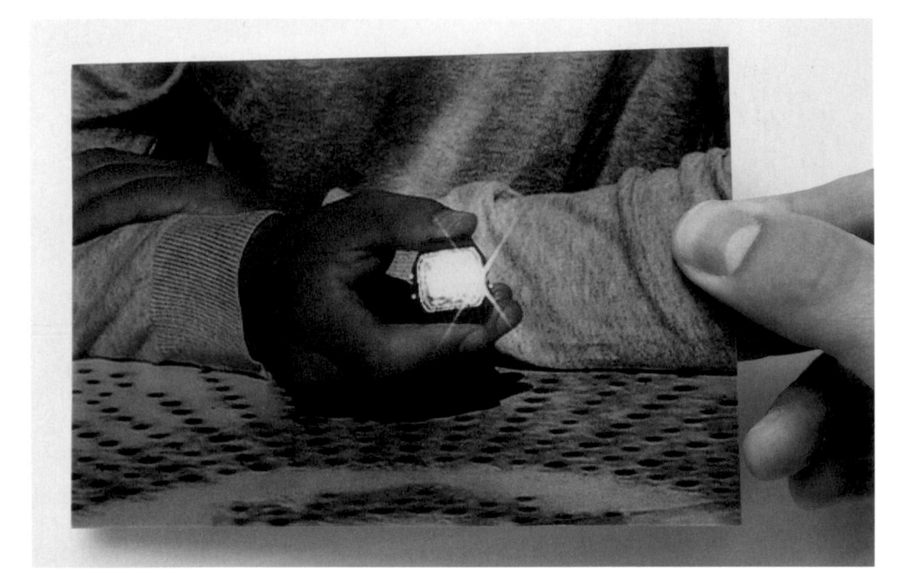

Casio 2007 / Lenticular postcard / 14.8 x 10.5 cm

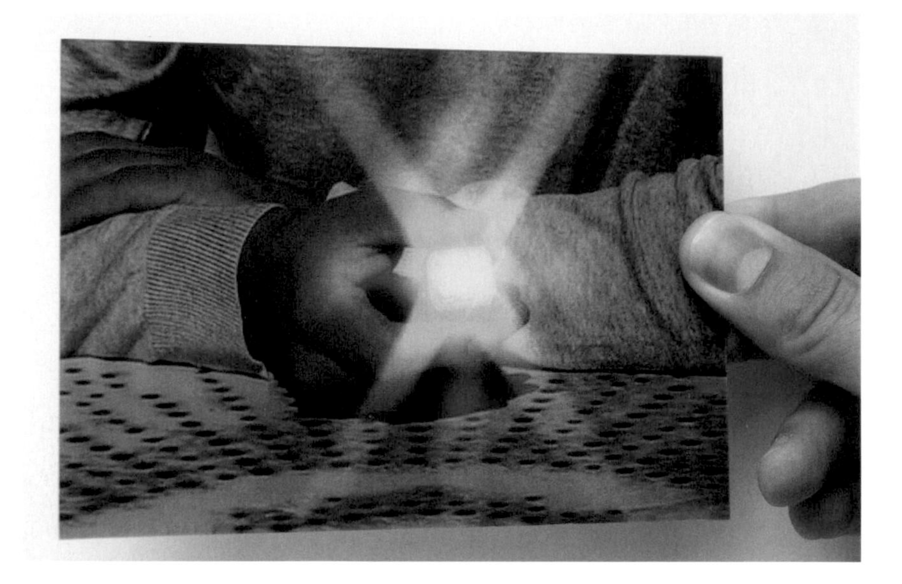

page 24–27 **Teleidoscope** 2007 / Car mounted teleidoscope / 61 x 61 x 61 x 122 cm

Smile 2007 / Freestanding barriers, elasticated cord / 40cm high, width variable

Biography

1971
Born Bangor, North Wales

2000–3
University College, Falmouth

2003–5
Slade School of Fine Art,
University College London

Selected exhibitions

2007
Some Vacant Accommodation,
Stroud Artspace

S.A.W. Show,
Finn Collective, Glasgow

OUTPOST presents British & European Legs,
Anglia Square Shopping Centre, Norwich

Art Now Cornwall, Tate St Ives

2006
Jonty Lees, New Work,
MOOT Nottingham (Solo)

2005
Invasions of Piquancy,
Kenny Schacter ROVE, London

LOOP Video Festival,
Barcelona, Spain

Somewhere In-between,
Galleri KiT, Trondheim, Norway

2004
Sounding Out Festival,
University East London

2003
Transitions 3,
Newlyn Art Gallery

List of works in show

All works courtesy the Artist

Tour de Studio
2007
Video
Duration 02:45:02

Untitled
2007
Video
Duration 12:31:22

Untitled
2007
Video
Duration 03:18:15

Casio
2007
Lenticular postcard
14.8 x 10.5 cm

We salute you!
2007
Assorted objects,
fishing wire, hooks
Dimensions variable

Untitled
2007
BMX bicycle, synthetic hair
Dimensions variable

cover image **We salute you!** 2007 / Assorted objects, fishing wire, hooks / Dimensions variable